Rotalever Revelator

Doug Nufer

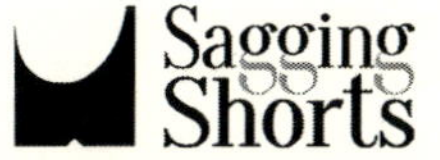

Printed in the United States of America.
Set in Doves Type with LaTeX.

ISBN: 978-1-952386-01-5 (paperback)
Library of Congress Control Number: 2020904229

Sagging Meniscus Press
Montclair, New Jersey
saggingmeniscus.com

Table of Illustrations

Used by kind permission of artist James Siena and Pace Gallery.

Rotalever Revelator

Rotalever Revelator

No Sam Mason or, eh, hero illuminati,
I tan, I mull, I, Rotalever Revelator
Spin nips, lap pal laid dial spool loops

I, maw's swami, baffle elf fab
Decal-laced revelator rot, a lever revel,
A tor rotalever revelator award
Draw a traced decart rat ava avatar loops
Spool spin nips

I, goy yogi, ren rut turner, avid diva
Recap pacer, spool loops, report troper
Elf fab baffle, emit time, edit tide
Teleport tropelet rot sap pastor
Straw warts, denonte e-toned sung gnus
Know wonk data a tad,
Crank radial laid ark narc rats star.

I tan, I mull, I
Illuminati avatar
Rat ava or, eh, hero
Revel at or rotalever
Reward drawer bin nib
Red now wonder
Spoons snoops

Rotalever Revelator

Retroper Reporter

Murmur rum rum, retroper reporter
Re-drum murder.

Rue sop poseur
Timid dim it tips spit
Parrot tor rap nips spin, pilfer
Reflip spacer recaps
Deliver reviled par rap per rep
Retroper reporter star rats.

Star rats know wonk lab rev
Verbal straw warts retool looter folio
Oil of generous sou reneg sung gnus

Retroper reporter star rats flog golf
Tang gnat spool loops.

Avid diva star rats edit tide
Leer, reel, recap pacer liar rail
Lapdog god pal
Sung gnus.

Retroper reporter

Animal Lamina

O cat taco
Reed deer
Pets step

A nut tuna
Alligator rot a gill a lee eel

Elba's sable
Sung gnus parrot tor rap

Gnat tang a mall llama
Cod doc

Dog god wolf flow
Dray yard oxen Nexo

Animal lamina

Etna Ante

Wolf rev overflow sun
rob born us lava
Aval mire volcano

On a clover
I'm all in
Wager re: gaw nil

La erupter
Ret pure
Sicilian nail

I, cis sic cis Isis sis,
I am gam magma

Tap pat, top pot
Ante Etna

Aval lava
Overflow
Wolf rev, O

Etna ante

Stressed Desserts

Edam made
Oil of folio
Set rot tortes

Stressed desserts
Tug gut tacos
So cat pans snap
A nut tuna
A crab barca

Sugar ragus
Regal lager soda ados
Rebut tuber

Pin rut turnip walnuts
Stun law embargos

So grab me, aromas
Sam or a rot cod doctor
REM may yammer

Deliver reviled gnat tang

Stressed desserts

Esnes Sense

Esnes sense knar rank bondage
Egad nob animus
Sum in a spin
Rut turnips, porcini
In I crop dirt
Up putrid flora
A rolf or rub

Burro, dig up
Pug id dismay yams
I'd sense esnes
Deliver reviled

Dray yard ox
XO slag gals snub
Buns sag gas soda ados
Ruffle elf fur
Batten net tab
Spam supper
Rep pus maps
Burg grub

Esne-fed defense welfare
Era flew
Repaid diaper generous sou reneg
Reknit tinker stink knits
Tapir rip at rat tar yap pay

Bus sub robalo
O labor puto or
Root up yam
May sense esnes

Esnes sense

Doom Mood

Warsaw was raw
Illuminati, I tan I mull I murmur
Rum rum red rum murder
Re-drum murder

I raki rah hari-kari
Mini-in, I'm alive
Evil, a pus sot tossup
O drat tardo dirge, e.g.
Rid raw war

O, rue Euro
Warsaw was raw

Snug guns abandon, nod, nab a
Damned den mad pariah

Ha! I rap snit tins tin mad, damn it
Deus sued DEO OED dog god spool loops

Finis sin if Nemo omen sub
Bus loops spool torii

I, I rot, devil lived
Ha, I rap pariah
Ho ho
Oh oh

Doom mood

Flog Golf

Flog golf
O, flog golfo
Pool loop spin nips
Snip pins, ram, mar
Murder, re-drum sports, strops

Strop ports embargo
O grab me, barger
Regrab strap parts
Wallop poll aw, stun law walnuts
Stun nuts, gnaw wang, mutilate, et. al. it, um

Flog golf
Rap par
Raps spar bonk knob
Pals slap, spit on no tips
Repel leper elf fur
Ruffle rat tar

Tar rat star rats sin
Net tennis bat tab
Bats stab red rum murder
Tackle elk cat naps, span

K.O. O.K.
O lop polo rapper rep par
Flor rolf, meh, yam mayhem
Of log golfo
Golf flog

Flog golf

romatibisubitomotibusibitamor
oromatibisubitomotibusibitamo
moromatibisubitomotibusibitam
amoromatibisubitomotibusibita
tamoromatibisubitomotibusibit
itamoromatibisubitomotibusibi
bitamoromatibisubitomotibusib
ibitamoromatibisubitomotibusi
sibitamoromatibisubitomotibus
usibitamoromatibisubitomotibu
busibitamoromatibisubitomotib
ibusibitamoromatibisubitomoti
tibusibitamoromatibisubitomot
otibusibitamoromatibisubitomo
motibusibitamoromatibisubitom
omotibusibitamoromatibisubito
tomotibusibitamoromatibisubit
itomotibusibitamoromatibisubi
bitomotibusibitamoromatibisub
ubitomotibusibitamoromatibisu
subitomotibusibitamoromatibis
isubitomotibusibitamoromatibi
bisubitomotibusibitamoromatib
ibisubitomotibusibitamoromati
tibisubitomotibusibitamoromat
atibisubitomotibusibitamoroma
matibisubitomotibusibitamorom
omatibisubitomotibusibitamoro
romatibisubitomotibusibitamor

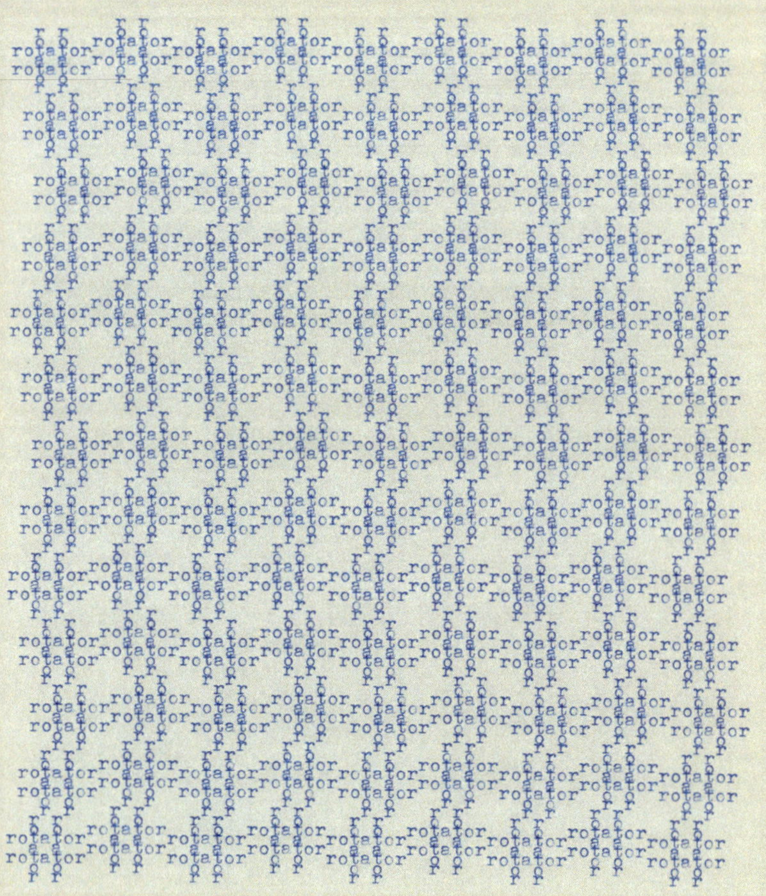

Rail Liar

Subway yaw bus rail liar
Parrot tor rap lab rev
Verbal noise hoc cohesion

Retool looter strap parts
Pilfer, reflip oil of folio
Tram mart

Smart trams
Alias sail a skow
Woks nab, rub us
Suburban rat-raced
Decar tar martini in
I tram reb baggage car
Race gag gabber spins

Snips ate ETA smart trams
Remit timer tubed debut
Poseur rue sop rap par
Tor rap parrot laid dial garb
Brag, laud dual elf-fab baffle

Degas sap-passaged folio
Oil of rail liar
Yaw bus subway
Smart trams

Rail liar

Mad Dam

Madam Ma dam
I, I rot torii
Tarbela ale brat
Gardiner ren I drag
A ram as samara
No sir rag Garrison
Guri, I rug Hoover
Rev ooh

O, I ho Ohio
Camo top Potomac
Era waled Delaware
Re: gin Niger at alp Plata

Golfo of log loop pool
Stopper rep pots
Woks skow wolf flow taps spat

Edit tide, seep pees
Kayak level reviver
Alee eel a Noel lag galleon Ahab

Bah, a tug gut
Alias sail a gob bog moor room
Net tab batten

But tub alligator rot a gill a
No is net tension

Ha ha, ah ah
Mini in, I'm nuts
Stun ria air, damn it

Tin mad
Mad dam

God Dog

Spot tops Zeus
Suez wolf flow spans
Snaps superstition

No, it its rep us Bostons
Snot sob dog god damned den mad
Ululator rot, a lulu
Nemo omen Nema amen

Borzoi I, Oz, rob
Yahweh, hew hay, snap
Pan's battle elt tab

Torah ha rot
Paws swap
Gnaw wang, ruffle elf fur

Allah hall, a mug gum
Pug gup spaniel lei naps
Ruffles self fur

God dog

O Rue Euro

Ria air déborder red-robed
Der red Bardolino
On I, lo drab

Niebla Albe
In dernier rein
Red Atem
Meta Roma Amor

Será Ares émaner, rename
Oder redo Marsala
Alas, ram Neptuno
O nut pen garçon
No crag Krabbe
Ebb ark Etna ante

Barco
O crab, débuter retubed
Roussel Lessuor RV VR
Verderb, bred rev
Enoteca acetone

O Rue Euro

Ria Air

Ria air
Niebla Albe in Barcelona
An olé crab
O crab Barco
Ram mar Ares
Será Neptuno

O nut pen de lodo
O doled ram
Golfo of log maritimo

Omit?
I ram Rio de la Plata

At alp, a led oir
Ay alp playa
Air tap patria rap par

Neptuno
O nut pen eel
Lee sani-gap páginas
So dot todos on at nap pantano
Sop mac campos

Días said ram led
Del mar

Ria air

Der Red

Tor rot der red rot tor Höhe
Eh, oh
Husten nets
Uh, Eiter
Re-tie oder redo Verderb
Bred-rev Atem meta Ruf.

Fur, das sad tot tot Tier re: it,
Später retaps das sad Mähne.

Enham, war raw, was, saw?
Net-ad-lose-id
Die Soldaten flow, rew,

Werwolf Krabbe ebb ark
Flug gulf Manöver
Rev on.

Am irre, err I
Der red rot Tor.

Der red

d'Écart Traced

d'écart traced
le bal lable délit
tiled mur rum gager
re-gag pis

sip défini
in I fed
definitif

Fit in, I fed par rap majeur
Rue jam
Débuter retubed
Déborder red-robed
Dénoter retoned metier re: item
Dernier rein
Red, truc, curt garçon

No crag foi
I of le trac cartel broder
red-orb
gêner, reneg, éditer re: tide

Mais Siam parc crap
Dada a dad
Mal lam
Finit tin if émaner rename
d'écart traced
Écarter retrace

d'Écart traced

RV VR

Maori, I roam
Sub in
I'm minibus Tioga
A go it Tioga ago
It, Nomad damon
Monaco oca nom
La roulotte et tolu oral
Artiste et Sitra Roussel
Lessuor, stallion noil lats

No Siam maison, la roulotte
Et tolu oral
Portable Elba
Trop rev or rover Maori

I roam Monaco
Oca nom et tulo oral
La roulotte
Noil lats stallion
Lessuor Roussel
Artiste et Sitra

RV VR

Vini in IV

Enoteca acetone
In IV vini
Asti, it's a cod DOC zona
An Oz
A jag
Gaja vino on IV

In IV
Vini Est Est Est
Tse tse tse
Vino di tavola
A lo vat I'd
On IV Marsala
Alas, ram

A ran it tag Gattinara
An O rev Verona
An if ur Rufina
Roma Amor.

Bardolino, on I lo drab
Passito, O tis sap
Recioto oto-icer

Garganega, age
Nag, rag

Pinot nero, O rent, O nip
Ante Etna vini in IV

Enoteca acetone
Vini in IV

Doctor Rotcod

Doctor Rotcod stressed desserts
Damned den mad star rats

Sugar ragus rebut tuber
Trader red art folios, soil of woks,
Skow walnuts, stun law snoops,
Spoons, spacer recaps.

Dog god doc cod, a nut tuna
On no ref log golfer patron
Nor tap a goy yoga,
Peed deep.

A ria air a diva avid aria air
A sung gnus aga's saga
A mall llama
Denoted detoned
At ad data
Six ax x-axis
Strap parts

Part trap arena
An era doom mood
Laced decal stink knits.

Trap A apart, reknit tinker
Lived devil live evil
Draw yaw wayward
Aloof fool
A moron, nor
Om meditator rot at idem item met,
I deflowered dere wolfed over rev
O revolver
Rev lover.

Evasion, no. I save
Net tab batten
Alias sail a sloop
Pools support trop pus,
Overflow wolf rev
O flog golfo of log, matey
Yet am I tan? I mull
I, illuminati,
Am all llama sage, e.g.
As amid dim a baffle
Elf fab gossamer
REM as sog gob bog
Pool loop yaws sway.

Am I Kay Yakima?
I pit tipi spans
Snaps Nez Zen red rum murder;
Re-drum murder tom-tom.

Mot mot parrot tor rap spar raps
De-reflip pilfered animal lamina elf fur
Ruffle on no patron nor tap Shaman Nam ahs.

I'm, alas, salami
A goy yoga origami
I'm a giro hero
Or, eh, no sam Mason.
Mini-in, I'm Marconi
In no cram pun rut turn
Up dial laid spin nips.

DJ JD am I: I'm a rapper
Rep par bogie man, name I gob
Snot tons
Snub buns
Gnus sung nuts stun.
Walnuts stun law
A la mode operandi

I'd nare P.O. Edom
A la nut tun martinis.

Sin I tram
Sleep peels
On a subway yaw bus
A no stops spots reel,
Leer at ad data,
Teleport tropelet patter
Ret tap part trap
Fiber reb if rabbinical
Laci nib bar
Now won.

Not now
Won-ton macaroni,
I nor a cam
Murmur rum rum tiki
I kit re-drum murder
Ratatat tatatar.
Mix a lot to lax,
I'm aroma
Am ora gas sag saga
Aga's defecation
No it ace fed apron
Nor Pa nor tap patron.

Alligator rot a gill a
Lamina animal
Deli I led a mall
Llama no sib bison
I daw wadi.

I O.K. koi,
Yo yo oy oy
I pit tipi citadels
Sled a tic self fur ruffles

To rebut tube rot animal
Lam in a dog god.

Eros sore
Siri Iris
Castor rot sac
A la sun orc Cronus
A la sum om Momus
Pan nap Ares será
Atlas salt a Zeus Suez
No die sop Posiedon
No die sop Poseidon
Zeus Suez.

Rot cod doctor
Doctor Rotcod Doctor Rotcod Doctor Rotcod

Doctor Rotcod

A to Z Zota

Avid diva
Bard drab
Caw WAC
Diaper repaid
Embargo, O grab me
Flor rolf
Generous sou reneg
Ha ha ah ah
Idol Lodi
Jar raj
Knar rank
Lager regal
Murmur rum rum
Nomad damon
Ogre ergo
Poseur rue sop
Quatar rat AQ
Rail liar
Snoops Spoons
Tips spit
Ubu
Viva Aviv
War raw
X-axis six ax
Yap pay
Zota A to Z

A to Z Zota

One Vowels Slew Oven O

Saga agas teem, meet, stink
Knits spool, loops murmur rum rum

Salal la-las peek, keep mini-in
I'm on no dub bud sag gas Zen

Nez, I pit tipi golf, flog smug gums
Par rap net ten tips, spit now won sung gnus

Parts strap, repel leper
Snit tins tor rot
Buns snub warts

Straw stressed desserts
I kit tiki nod don mumu um um
Tarp prat esne-fed defense knits stink,
Look Kool tub but knar rank

Keels sleek sic cis tons
Snot nuts stun

One Vowels Slew Oven O

Sonnet Ten Nos

Nebraska oxen animus baton
Med aid abandon doctor diadem
Deflower Barcelona lone idem
Nuts Lana Turner galleon strap on
Flow nab rub us pud exes trope let don
Snub garb drawer decal A to Z live wen
Wolf animus evangel my nope Zen
Stressed doctor Eros Patron tug wang on

Refed sin if rue sop e-toned flog sung
Enola bomber defense lever pool
Eloped evasion alligator won
Refer deb me to do embargo tool
Revamp emit reward deliver time
Deport damned animus Nebraska dial.

Sonnet Ten Nos

Lingos Sog Nil

Okefenokee eek
One Fe K.O.
Iron nori bog gob
Room moor pool loop

Deep maws swam, peed
Par rap patois
Sí, O tap sog nil lingos
Denim mired Dismal lams I'd
Deport, troped mud dum
Alligator rot
A gill a tapir
Rip at swamp-rat
Tarp maws

Gob bog iron
Nori, eek one Fe
K.O. Okefenokee
Lams I'd
Dismal retroper reporter
Loop, pool, slog nil lingos

Lingos sog nil

Spawned Den Waps

Spawned den waps
Tridymites
Seti, my dirt
Illuminati
I tan I mull I

Embed deb me
Origami, I'm a giro
Tetrabasic cis a bar Tet

Cohesion noise hoc
Bogie man name I gob
Tradition. No, it I dart

Ruffle elf fur
Animus sum in a
Macaroni, in or a cam

Evangel leg nave citadel.
Led, a tic trepanation?

No, I tan, nap pert.

Spawned den waps

Set, a Name Emanates

Atlas Salta, atlas coda, a doc's alta
Spam maps are era sports strops
Raps spar a la trader,
Re-dart trader red art

My nope eponym
Re: fun Nufer
Set, a name emanates

Toil EST, T.S. Eliot
Toil est. T.S. Eliot
Leer reel star rats
Literati I tare til
Camus Sumac turn up pun, rut
Sumac Camus

Set, a name emanates

Trader Red Art

Visa as IV
Yahoo oo hay Paypal lap yap
Aflac calf a Nexo oxen

Petsmart tram step Walmart tram law
Dominos son I'm o.d. Hardee's seed rah
Tacotime emit O cat Panda ad nap
Arby's sybra Subway yaw bus

Subaru ur a bus Airbus sub ria
Delta at led Rover rev or
Avis Siva Yamaha aha may

Peets steep Bud dub
Dom Perignon non GI rep mod Kool
Look, Seven-Up pun, Eve's
Dr. Pepper rep pep rd. Pepsi is pep

Adidas sad id a
Samsung gnu's Ma's
X-finity y tin if x
Disney yens' id

Trader red art

R O M A T I B I S U B I T O M O T I B U S I B I T A M O R

R O M A T I B I S U B I T O M O T I B U S I B I T A M O

R R O M A T I B I S U B I T O M O T I B U S I B I T A M O

R R O M A T I B I S U B I T O M O T I B U S I B I T A M

O R R O M A T I B I S U B I T O M O T I B U S I B I T A M

O R R O M A T I B I S U B I T O M O T I B U S I B I T A

M O R R O M A T I B I S U B I T O M O T I B U S I B I T A

M O R R O M A T I B I S U B I T O M O T I B U S I B I T

A M O R R O M A T I B I S U B I T O M O T I B U S I B I T

A M O R R O M A T I B I S U B I T O M O T I B U S I B I

T A M O R R O M A T I B I S U B I T O M O T I B U S I B I

T A M O R R O M A T I B I S U B I T O M O T I B U S I B

I T A M O R R O M A T I B I S U B I T O M O T I B U S I B

I T A M O R R O M A T I B I S U B I T O M O T I B U S I

B I T A M O R R O M A T I B I S U B I T O M O T I B U S I

B I T A M O R R O M A T I B I S U B I T O M O T I B U S

I B I T A M O R R O M A T I B I S U B I T O M O T I B U S

I B I T A M O R R O M A T I B I S U B I T O M O T I B U

S I B I T A M O R R O M A T I B I S U B I T O M O T I B U

S I B I T A M O R R O M A T I B I S U B I T O M O T I B

U S I B I T A M O R R O M A T I B I S U B I T O M O T I B

U S I B I T A M O R R O M A T I B I S U B I T O M O T I

B U S I B I T A M O R R O M A T I B I S U B I T O M O T I

B U S I B I T A M O R R O M A T I B I S U B I T O M O T

I B U S I B I T A M O R R O M A T I B I S U B I T O M O T

I B U S I B I T A M O R R O M A T I B I S U B I T O M O

T I B U S I B I T A M O R R O M A T I B I S U B I T O M O

T I B U S I B I T A M O R R O M A T I B I S U B I T O M

O T I B U S I B I T A M O R R O M A T I B I S U B I T O M

O T I B U S I B I T A M O R R O M A T I B I S U B I T O

M O T I B U S I B I T A M O R R O M A T I B I S U B I T O

M O T I B U S I B I T A M O R R O M A T I B I S U B I T

O M O T I B U S I B I T A M O R R O M A T I B I S U B I T

O M O T I B U S I B I T A M O R R O M A T I B I S U B I

T O M O T I B U S I B I T A M O R R O M A T I B I S U B I

T O M O T I B   S I B I T A M O R R O M A T I B I S U B

I T O M O T I B U S I B I T A M O R R O M A T I B I S U B

I T O M O T I B U S I B I T A M O R R O M A T I B I S U

B I T O M O T I B U S I B I   A M O R R O M A T I B I S U

B I T O M O T I B U S I B I T A M O R R O M A T I B I S

U B I T O M O T I B U S I B I T A M O R R O M A T I B I S

U B I T O M O T I B U S I B I T A M O R R O M A T I B I

S U B I T O M O T I B U S I B I T A M O R R O M A T I B I

S U B I T O M O T I B U S I B I T A M O R R O M A T I B

I S U B I T O M O T I B U S I B I T A M O R R O M A T I B

I S U B I T O M O T I B U S I B I T A   O   R O M A T I

B I S U B I T O M O T I B U S I B I T A M O R R O M A T I

B I S U B I T O M O T I B U S I B I T A M O R R O M A T

neveroddoreven

T.S. Eliot Toil, Est.

Emit time now won
Emit time over rev
O time emit anon
No na forever
Rever of now won
Agos sog a time, emit era
Are rever of forever
Abstraction? No it carts ba humbug
Gubmuh solos stun nuts
Nut tun solos are era ere won now

Pets step yo-yo oy oy a la reviver
On no yaw way ew we did
Leer, reel, resonate ETA noser
On no door rood Ned rages
Or rose-garden.
Raps spar, resonate ETA noser.

But tub re-cart tracer, pilfer
Reflip an era arena flora
A rolf on no wonk know.

Elf fab baffle noise hoc cohesion nips spin
"Trace, lure us, sue rule cart"
A robin nib or a parrot tor rap spar raps,
"Sue rule cart, trace, lure us."
Dare we, ewe rad, mar ram aloof,
Fool a tor rap parrot?

In on, non I, avis Siva avatar
Rat Ava Eve ere flew welfare
Stressed dessert's torte's set rot
Over rev, O tor rot, an I in a Roma Amor
Air ria parrot tor rap animal lamina
Cis um music self fab baffles
Eye fixes sex if

Finis sin if deflower rewolfed
Sore Eros saw, was a rolf flora
Deflower rewolfed.

Slap pals spar raps
We'd dew parts strap on no patron nor tap
Tradition. No, it I'd art traced
Decart decal laced spins, snips alley
Yell a border red rob alit til a
Sere ere's pool loop spools sloops maroon
No? Or am I daw wadi pool
Loop-deloop pooled, filled dell if lit
Til a lotos sot ola
Repaid diaper deep peed dew
We'd deliver reviled.
Now won, sub-min nimbus
Defer refed pool loop abandon.
"Nod, nab a bacon, no, cab,"
Tor rap parrot welfare era flew.

Star rats made Edam supper rep pus
Ergo ogre regal lager.
"Draw away, yaw award," tor rap parrot
Denoted, detoned.
"Smug gums pooh-pooh hoop-hoop
Sports strops."

Emit time over rev
O emit time anon
Non a forever rever of now
Won rever of forever

T.S. Eliot Toil, Est.

Leer Reel

Star rats sore Eros dew
Wed Ava Gardner
Rend Rag Ava
And DNA art anis knarf
Frank Sinatra
A la loo oolala
Nuts stun, buns snub
Put tup putt up Lana Turner
Ren rut anal on rope port
Trope porno bondage
Egad nob sap Pa's milf
Flim loop pool masturbator
Rot a brut Sam
Deflower rewolfed golf flog
Regit Tiger par rap Sharon Stone
Eton's Norah's avid diva
On I cap LA Al Pacino
Regrab barger lever revel snap
Pans debut, tubed wang gnaw
Liz Taylor roly at zil re-drum
Murder pees seep
A la loo oolala
Sexed-up pud exes
Trope porno on rope port
Rot a brut's AM masturbator

Leer reel

Sumac Camus

A coloratura soprano
On Arp osa ruta, ro loca
Teleport trope, let notes set on Marconi
In O cram le bal label, le ber rebel
Le bon Nobel rebel le ber Albert trebla Camus

Sumac, Yma Amy
Avid diva Camus Sumac
Aria air a verbal lab rev ululator
Rotalulu oratorio
Oir, O taro
Ay ay ay, ya ya ya oolala a la loo

Peste et sep, L'Etranger re-gnar tel
La sangre erg nasal a cito Xe

Exotica Andina
An I, DNA
Llama am all gnus sung scat tacs
No rey aces se cayeron
So los tacs scat solos
Amilanar rana Lima
Camus Sumac Amy Yma
Trebla Albert Camus Sumac

Sumac Camus

My Nope Eponym

Ada's sad a
Roma Amor Eros sore Casanova
Avon a sac Disney,
Yens I'd in no cram Marconi
In it, ram Martini
A rod nap Pandora
Napoleon Noe
Lop an Oedipus sup ideo
Spooner Reno ops news per reps wen
Sore Eros Iron Maiden Ned I am
Nor I Avon a sac Casanova

Madonna anno dam Adam mad
A Hoover rev ooh
Ada ad a Narcissus suss
I cran non GI rep mod
Dom Perignon Amor Roma
Ada's sad a

My Nope Eponym

Nufer Re: fun

Drab bard evasion?
No, I save my nope eponym
Strop sod Nuferism
Ms, I ref, undo sports
Ruffle elf fur, baffle elf fab
Leer, reel, brag garb
Wahoo oo haw, e.g.
A revel leverage

Lever revel
Regal lager, vino on IV, martini in it
Ram spins, snips ah ah
Ha ha narco, O cran
Reflip, pilfer rap
Par retroper reporter

Hedonism Ms? I nod, eh, O.K.
K.O. timer, remit
Refund D. Nufer salami
I'm alas, a memoir rio, me

Ma, amuse Esuma, Niger, re-gin
Sog, nil lingos
Leer, reel, baffle elf fab

Self fab baffles pilfer
Reflip spins snips

Nufer re:fun

Atlas Salta

Oir Rio
O flog Golfo of log
A Ma nap Panama
Ram mar ria, air Aruba
A bur a grub burg
Barcelona, an olé crab

O rue Euro paen neap tide
Edit Suez, Zeus
Not sob Boston
Nil bud Dublin
Lodi idol Aksarben, Nebraska

No VA Avon Eton note
Senegal LA genes

Asia a is a
Florida ad I rolf

Atlas Salta

Atlas Coda, A Doc's Alta

Bulgaria, air a glub
Viva, let Tel Aviv
Air a glub, Bulgaria

Warsaw was raw
Berlin nil reb
Bergen neg reb
Lima a mil
Bogotá at O gob

Napoli
I lop an Ontario
O, I rat on Miami
I maim Scranton, not narcs

Mali? I lam
Walla Walla all aw, all aw
Ohio O, I
Ho, Tuscon

Nos cut Sparta
At raps Saginaw.
Wan, I gas Ottawa
A Watt O
Erie Eire

Habana a nab
Ah Gabon
No, bag Niger
Re-gin Zamora
Aroma Z

Atlas coda, a doc's alta

Sports Strops

Mets stem
Yankees seek
Nay Cub Buc Pirates set a rip
Royal lay or Astros sorts:
A Marlin nil ram

Ram mar Bengals slag
Neb Lion noil

Net ten Sixer rex is
Pacer recap
Pistons snot sip

Sabers Serb as
Devil lived
Star rats

Sports strops

Revelator Rotalever

No Sam or, eh, illuminati
Rotalever spin lap laid spool,

I, maw's baffle, decal revelator, revel;
A tor rotalever award traced rat Ava pools' spin.

I, goy, ren rut avid, recap, spool, report elf fab
Emit, edit, teleport rot sap straw
Denote sung know data, crank radial rats.

I tan, I mull, I avatar or, eh, revelator
Reward bin red now spoons.

Denotation retroper murmur
Retroper re-drum rue sop timid tips
Parrot nips, pilfer spacer
Deliver par per retroper star.

Star, know lab rev straw, retool folio.
Generous sung retroper star flog tang spool.

Avid star, edit leer, recap liar
Lapdog sung animal.

Etna wolf rev
O

Ava mire volcano
All in wager erupter Sicilian
Sic I sis am gam tap top
Ante aval overflow Etna.

O rue ria,
Déborder der Bardolino
Niebla dernier Atem.
Roma será émaner oder Marsala

Neptuno garçon Krabbe Etna
Barco, débuter Roussel RV
Verderb enoteca.

Lateral doctor stressed damned star
Sugar rebut trader folios, woks
Walnuts snoops lingos.

Okefenokee iron bog room pool deep maws
Par patois sog nil mired lams I'd troped.
Dum mud rot a gill a rip at tarp maws.

Bog nori, Okefenokee
Dismal reporter pool lingos.

Spawned tridymites
Illuminati embed origami
Tetrabasic noise hoc
Name I gob?

No, it I dart
Set a name

Atlas, atlas, a doc spam
Are sports raps a la trader.

Trader, my nope
Re: fun set a name.

Toil EST, toil est.
Leer star literati
Camus turn up Sumac.

My nope, Ada's Ada
Roma Eros Casanova Disney.

Disney in no cram in it
Ram Pandora sup ideo.

Reno ops reps wen
Eros Ned I am
Nor I Casanova
Amor Ada's Ada.

My nope Nufer drab evasion?
My nope strop sod Nuferism
Ruffle, baffle leer, brag wahoo e.g.
A revel lager on IV
In it ram
Ha ha O cran
Pilfer par reporter.

Ms? I nod, eh, K.O., remit
D. Nufer I'm alas, rio me, Ma.

Lingos leer, baffle
Self fab baffle spins re: fun.

Revelator Rotalever

Doug Nufer's novels include *Lifeline Rule* (Spuyten Duyvil, 2015), *By Kelman Out of Pessoa* (Les Figues, 2011), *The Mudflat Man/The River Boys* (soultheft records, 2006), *On the Roast* (Chiasmus, 2004), *Negativeland* (Autonomedia, 2004), and *Never Again* (Black Square, 2004). He is the author of the poetry collections *The Me Theme* (Sagging Meniscus, 2017), *We Were Werewolves* (Make Now, 2008), *The Dammed* (ubu.com, 2011), and *Lounge Acts* (Insert Blanc, 2013). His most recent book is *Metamorphosis* (Sagging Meniscus, 2018), which changes forms. He sells wine in Seattle.

DEVIL NEVER EVEN LIVED
DEVIL NEVER EVEN LIVED
DEVIL NEVER EVEN LIVED
DEVIL NEVER EVEN LIVED

DEVIL NEVER EVEN LIVED
NEVER EVEN LIVED NEVER
EVEN LIVED DEVIL NEVER
LIVED DEVIL NEVER EVEN
NEVER NEVER EVEN LIVED
NEVER EVEN LIVED DEVIL
LIVED DEVIL NEVER EVEN
NEVER NEVER EVEN LIVED
NEVER EVEN LIVED DEVIL
EVEN LIVED DEVIL NEVER
LIVED DEVIL NEVER EVEN
DEVIL NEVER EVEN LIVED
NEVER EVEN LIVED DEVIL
EVEN LIVED DEVIL NEVER
LIVED DEVIL NEVER NEVER
EVEN LIVED DEVIL NEVER
LIVED DEVIL NEVER LIVED
DEVIL NEVER EVEN LIVED
NEVER NEVER LIVED LIVED
EVEN LIVED DEVIL NEVER
LIVED DEVIL NEVER EVEN
DEVIL NEVER EVEN LIVED
NEVER EVEN LIVED DEVIL
EVEN LIVED DEVIL NEVER
LIVED DEVIL NEVER LIVED
DEVIL NEVER EVEN LIVED
NEVER EVEN LIVED DEVIL
EVEN LIVED DEVIL NEVER
LIVED DEVIL NEVER EVEN
DEVIL NEVER EVEN LIVED
NEVER EVEN LIVED DEVIL
EVEN LIVED DEVIL NEVER
LIVED DEVIL NEVER LIVED
DEVIL NEVER EVEN LIVED
NEVER EVEN LIVED DEVIL
EVEN LIVED DEVIL NEVER
LIVED DEVIL NEVER EVEN
DEVIL NEVER EVEN LIVED
NEVER EVEN LIVED NEVER
EVEN LIVED DEVIL NEVER
LIVED DEVIL NEVER EVEN
DEVIL NEVER EVEN LIVED
NEVER EVEN LIVED DEVIL
EVEN LIVED DEVIL NEVER
LIVED DEVIL NEVER EVEN
DEVIL NEVER EVEN LIVED
EVEN LIVED DEVIL NEVER
LIVED DEVIL NEVER EVEN
DEVIL NEVER EVEN LIVED
NEVER EVEN LIVED DEVIL
EVEN LIVED DEVIL NEVER
DEVIL NEVER EVEN LIVED

Revelator Rotalever

Doug Nufer

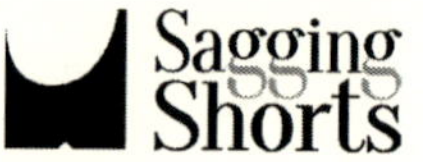

Revelator
Rotalever

Revelator Rotalever

Nufer snips, baffles
Elf fab reel sog nil.

A memoir salami refund timer
O.K., hedonism.

Retroper rap, reflip narco
Ah, ah
Martini, vino
Regal leverage, ooh.

Aw, garb, reel elf fab elf fur Ms.
I, re:fun, do sports.

Eponym? No, I save
Bard re:fun eponym.

Ada's Ada, Roma Avon
A sac iron maiden sore
News per Spooner
Oedipus
A rod nap Martini
Marconi, yen's id
Yens I'd Avon a sac sore Amor
Ada's Ada eponym.

Camus pun rut Sumac
I tare til rats reel T.S. Eliot.

T.S. Eliot emanates
Nufer eponym red art
Re-dart a la spar strops
Era maps coda salt a Salta
Emanates tradition.

Bogie man cohesion

Cis a bar Tet
I'm a giro, deb me,
I tan, I mull, I set.

I, my dirt den
Waps sog nil
Loop retroper lams I'd
Eek!
One Fe, K.O., iron gob.

Swamp-rat tapir, alligator
Dum mud deport Dismal
De-rim lingos, sí, O tap.

Rap swam, peed loop moor
Gob nori, Eek!
One Fe K.O. sog nil.

Spoons stun law, skow soil of red art
Tuber ragus, rats, den mad desserts
Rot, cod, Lar, et. al.

Acetone bred rev VR
Lessour retubed
O crab ante, ebb ark no crag
O nut pen, alas ram
Redo, rename Ares, Amor
Meta rein red Albe in, on
I, lo drab, red, red-robed air Euro.

Ante wolf rev, O lava Etna
Pot pat magma, sis, I cis nail
I cis ret pure re: gaw
Nil LA on a clover
I'm a VA
Overflow ante.

Lamina gnus god pal

Rail pacer, reel tide rats.

Diva loops gnat golf
Rats reporter gnus

Sou reneg oil of looter warts
Verbal wonk rats.

Rats reporter rep rap reviled recaps reflip spin
Tor rap spit dim it poseur murder reporter:
Rum rum reporter?
No, it atoned.

Snoops wonder nib drawer rot, a lever hero
Rat Ava illuminati star laid ark narc
A tad wonk gnus e-toned warts pastor trope
Let tide time baffle troper loops
Pacer diva turner yogi.

Nips spool avatar, decart
Draw a revelator
Rot a lever rotalever
Laced elf fab swami.

Loops dial pal nips
Revelator, I tan I mull
I hero mason.

Revelator Rotalever

Sports Strops

Star rats
Devil lived Sabers

Serb as Pistons
Snot sip Pacer Recap

Sixer rex is
Net ten
Lion noil

Bengals slag neb
Ram, mar Marlin nil
Ram Astros sorts

A Royal lay or
Pirates set a rip

Cub Buc Yankees seek
Nay Mets stem

Sports Strops

Atlas Coda, a Doc's Alta

Zamora aroma Z
Niger re-gin Gabon
No, bag Habana
A nab, ah

Erie Eire Ottawa
A Watt
O Saginaw
Wan, I gas Sparta
At raps

Tuscon nos cut Ohio
O, I
Ho, Walla Walla
All aw, all aw

Scranton not narcs' Miami
I maim Ontario
O, I rat on Napoli

I lo pan Bogotá
At O gob Lima
A mil Bergen

Neg reb Berlin
Nil reb Warsaw
Was raw air

A glub Bulgaria

Viva, let Tel Aviv, Bulgaria
Air a glub

Atlas Coda, a Doc's Alta

Atlas Salta

Florida ad
I rolf Asia
A is A

Senegal
LA genes, Eton
Note no VA Avon

Aksarben, Nebraska
Lodi idol
Nil bud Dublin not
Sob Boston

Suez
Zeus tide
Edit paen neap
O rue Euro

Barcelona, an olé crab grub burg
Aruba a bur
A ria air ram

Mar a Ma nap Panama
Golfo of log golf
O Oir Rio

Atlas Salta

Nufer Re: fun

Spins, snips pilfer, reflip
Self fab baffles

Baffle elf fab, leer, reel
Sog nil lingos
Niger re: gin
Amuse Esuma

A memoir rio, me
Ma salami, I'm, alas
Refund D. Nufer

Timer, remit, O.K.?
K.O. hedonism, Ms.
I nod, eh

Retroper reporter
Rap par reflip
Pilfer narco, O cran
Ah ah ha ha spins snips

Martini in it, ram vino on IV
Regal lager lever revel. e.g.
A revel leverage

Wahoo, ooh, aw
Brag garb leer, reel
Baffle elf fab, ruffle elf fur, strop sod

Nuferism, Ms., I ref, undo sports

My nope eponym evasion?
No, I save drab bard

Nufer Re: fun

My Nope Eponym

Ad ass Ada
Amor Roma
Non GI rep mod Dom Perignon
Narcissus suss, I cran

Ada ad a Hoover rev ooh
Adam mad a
Madonna anno dam Avon
A sac Casanova

Iron maiden
Ned I am nor I
Sore Eros

News per reps wen
Spooner Reno ops
Oedipus sup ideo
Napoleon Noel
O pan a rod nap Pandora

In it ram
Martini in no cram Marconi
Disney yen's id Casanova
Avon a sac
Eros sore Roma Amor
Ada's sad a

My Nope Eponym

Sumac Camus

Camus Sumac, trebla Albert
Amy Yma Camus Sumac

Amilanar rana Lima
So los tacs scat solos
No rey aces se cayeron

Scat tacs gnus
Sung llama

Am all Andina an I DNA
A cito Xe exotica

La sangre erg nasal
L'Etranger re-gnar tel
Peste et sep

Oolala a la loo ay ay ay ya ya ya
Oratorio oir O taro ululator

Rotalulu verbal lab rev aria
Air a Camus Sumac avid diva
Yma Amy Camus Sumac

Albert Trebla rebel
Le ber le bon Nobel
Le ber rebel le bal label

Marconi in O cram notes
Set on, teleport trope

Let a coloratura soprano
On Arp osa ruta ro loca

Sumac Camus

Leer Reel

Rot a brut Sam masturbator
Trope porno on rope port

Sexed-up pud exes
A la loo oolala

Pees seep, red rum murder
Liz Taylor, roly at zil wang gnaw

Debut tubed, snap Pan's lever revel
Regrab barger on I cap LA Al Pacino

Avid diva Sharon Stone
Eton's Norah's par rap regit Tiger golf flog
Deflower rewolfed masturbator

Rot a brut Sam, loop pool milf flim sap
Pa's bondage
Egad nob on rope port trope porno

Lana Turner, ren rut anal
Put tup putt up buns snub nuts stun

A la loo oolala art anis knarf
Frank Sinatra and DNA Ava Gardner

Rend rag Ava dew wed
Sore Eros star rats

Leer Reel

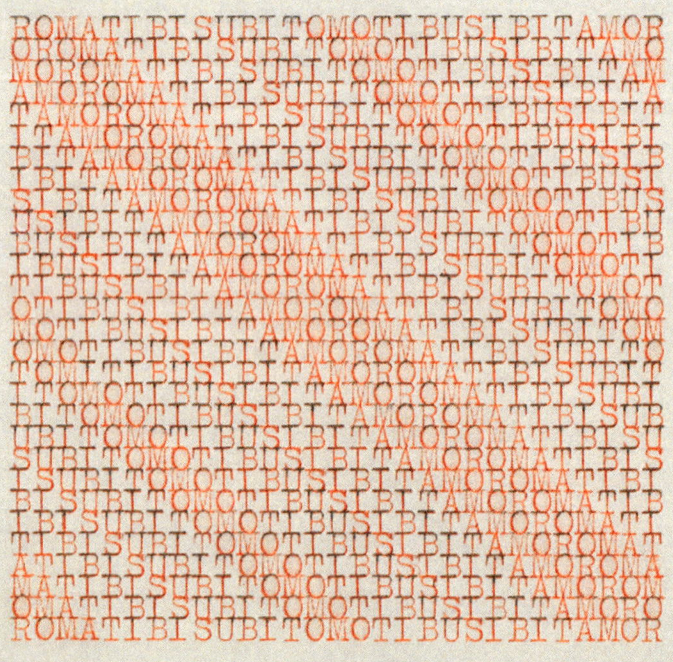
ROMATIBISUBITOMOTIBUSIBITAMOR
OROMATIBISUBITOMOTIBUSIBITAMO
MOROMATIBISUBITOMOTIBUSIBITAM
AMOROMATIBISUBITOMOTIBUSIBITA
TAMOROMATIBISUBITOMOTIBUSIBIT
ITAMOROMATIBISUBITOMOTIBUSIBI
BITAMOROMATIBISUBITOMOTIBUSIB
IBITAMOROMATIBISUBITOMOTIBUSI
SIBITAMOROMATIBISUBITOMOTIBUS
USIBITAMOROMATIBISUBITOMOTIBU
BUSIBITAMOROMATIBISUBITOMOTIB
IBUSIBITAMOROMATIBISUBITOMOTI
TIBUSIBITAMOROMATIBISUBITOMOT
OTIBUSIBITAMOROMATIBISUBITOMO
MOTIBUSIBITAMOROMATIBISUBITOM
OMOTIBUSIBITAMOROMATIBISUBITO
TOMOTIBUSIBITAMOROMATIBISUBIT
ITOMOTIBUSIBITAMOROMATIBISUBI
BITOMOTIBUSIBITAMOROMATIBISUB
UBITOMOTIBUSIBITAMOROMATIBISU
SUBITOMOTIBUSIBITAMOROMATIBIS
ISUBITOMOTIBUSIBITAMOROMATIBI
BISUBITOMOTIBUSIBITAMOROMATIB
IBISUBITOMOTIBUSIBITAMOROMATI
TIBISUBITOMOTIBUSIBITAMOROMAT
ATIBISUBITOMOTIBUSIBITAMOROMA
MATIBISUBITOMOTIBUSIBITAMOROM
OMATIBISUBITOMOTIBUSIBITAMORO
ROMATIBISUBITOMOTIBUSIBITAMOR

rotatoreifierotatoreifierotatoreifierotatoreifierotatoreifier

T.S. Eliot Toil, Est.

Rever of forever now won
Forever rever of anon
No, na emit time over rev
O emit time.

"Sports strops pooh-pooh
Hoop-hoop smug gums,"
Denoted, detoned tor rap parrot.
"Draw away yaw, award."

Regal lager ergo ogre supper rep pus
Made Edam star rats.

Welfare era flew tor rap parrot,
"Bacon, no, cab, abandon."
Nod nab a pool loop, defer refed
Sub-min nimbus now won.
Deliver reviled dew we'd
Deep peed, repaid diaper.
A lotos sot ola lit til filled dell
If de-loop pooled pool loop.
I, daw wadi maroon, no or
Am spools, sloops pool loop
Sere ere's alit til a border red
Rob alley yell a spin's snips
Decal laced traced de-cart tradition.
No, it I'd art patron
Nor tap on no parts strap
Wed dew spar raps
Slap pals.

Deflower rewolfed, a rolf flora
Saw, was sore Eros.
Deflower rewolfed finis sin
If fixes sex
If eye self fab baffles cis um music

Animal lamina parrot tor rap
Air ria Roma Amor
An I in a tor rot
Over rev O
Tortes set, rot
Stressed desserts' era flew welfare
Eve avatar rat Ava
Avis Siva in on non I.

Tor rap parrot aloof, fool a mar ram,
Dare we ewer ad?
"Sue, rule cart, trace, lure us," spar raps
Parrot tor rap a robin nib or a trace,
"Lure us, sue rule cart."
Nips spin noise hoc cohesion
Elf fab baffle.

Wonk know on no flora
A rolf, an era arena
Pilfer, reflip, re-cart tracer
But tub resonate ETA noser raps spar.

Ned rages or rosegarden door rood
On NO resonate, ETA noser.
Leer, reel.
Did ew we yaw way on no reviver
A la yo-yo oy oy pets step.

Won now ere are era solos, nut tun stun nuts solos, humbug
Gubmuh abstraction? No, it carts
Bar ever of forever era.
Are time emit agos a sog now won forever?
Rever of anon, no na time emit over rev
O emit time now won, emit time.

T.S. Eliot Toil, Est.

Trader Red Art

Disney yens' id
X-finity y tin if x Samsung
Gnu's Ma's Adidas
Sad id.

A Pepsi is pep
Dr. Pepper Reppep Rd.
Seven-Up pun, Eve's Kool look
Dom Perignon non GI rep
Mod Bud dub
Peets steep

Yamaha a ham ay
Avis Siva Rover rev or
Delta at led Airbus
Sub ria Subaru
Ur a bus

Subway yaw bus
Arby's sybra Panda ad nap
Tacotime, emit
O, cat Hardee's seed rah
Domino's son, I'm
O.D. Walmart tram law
Petsmart tram step

Nexo oxen, Aflac calf a
Paypal lap
Yap Yahoo ooh ay
Visa as IV

Trader Red Art

Set, a Name Emanates

Sumac Camus
Turn up pun
Rut Camus Sumac
Literati I tare til
Star rats leer, reel, toil
EST T.S. Eliot
Toil est. T.S. Eliot

Set, a name emanates
Re: fun Nufer
My nope eponym

Trader red art
Trader re-dart a la raps spar
Sports strops are era spam maps

Atlas coda, a doc's alta
Atlas Salta

Set. a name emanates

Spawned Den Waps

Trepanation?
No, I tan, a pert citadel.
Led, a tic evangel
Leg nave Marconi
In or a cam animus
Sum in a ruffle

Elf fur tradition?
No, it I dart.

Bogie man name
I gob cohesion noise hoc

Tetrabasic
Cis a bar Tet
Origami, I'm a giro

Embed deb me
Illuminati
I tan I mull I, tridymites
Seti my dirt

Spawned den waps

Lingos Sog Nil

Sog nil lingos loop
Pool retroper reporter
Lams I'd
Dismal, eek!
One Fe K.O.
Okefenokee
Iron nori gob bog

Swamp-rat tarp maws
Tapir rip at
Alligator rot
A gill a mud dum

Deport troped Dismal lams
I'd, denim mired, sog
Nil lingos patios
Si, O tap par rap
Deep maws swam, peed

Pool loop room moor
Bog gob iron nori
Okefenokee
Eek!
One Fe K.O.

Lingos sog nil

Sonnet Ten Nos

Laid Aksarben sum in a den mad troped
Emit reviled drawer time PM aver
Loot O grab me O dot embed refer
Now rot a gill a no I save depole
Loop revel esne-fed reb mob alone
Gnus golf detone poseur finis defer
No gnaw gut nor tap sore rot cod desserts
Nez eponym leg nave sum in a flow

New evil Zota laced reward brag buns
Nod teleport sexed-up suburban wolf
No parts Noel lag ren rut anal stun
Medi enol an ole crab rewolfed
Med aid rot cod nod nab a diadem
No tab sum in a Nexo Aksarben.

Sonnet Ten Nos

One Vowels Slew Oven O

Nuts stun
Tons snot
Sic cis
Keels sleek
Knar rank

Tub but
Look Kool
Knits stink
Esne-fed defense
Tarp prat

Mumu um um
Nod don
I kit tiki
Stressed desserts
Warts straw

Buns snub
Tor rot
Snit tins
Repel leper
Parts strap

Sung gnus now won tips spit net ten par rap
Smug gums golf flog I pit tipi Zen Nez sag gas

Dub bud on no mini-in I'm peek keep salal la-las
Murmur rum rum spool loops stink knits teem meet saga agas

One Vowels Slew Oven O

A to Z Zota

Zota A to Z
Yap pay
X-axis six ax
War raw
Viva Aviv

Ubu
Tips spit
Snoops spoons
Rail liar
Quatar rat AQ

Poseur rue sop
Ogre ergo
Nomad damon
Murmur rum rum
Lager regal
Knar rank
Jar raj
Idol Lodi
Ha ha ah ah

Generous sou reneg
Flor rolf
Embargo O grab me

Diaper repaid
Caw WAC
Bard drab
Avid diva

A to Z Zota

Doctor Rotcod

Doctor Rotcod Doctor Rodcod Doctor Rotcod
Rot cod doctor Zeus Suez
No die sop Poseidon
No die sop Poseidon Zeus Suez
Atlas Salta Ares será
Pan nap sum om Momus
A la sun orc Cronus
A la Castor rot sac Siri Iris
Eros sore dog god
Animal lamina
To rebut tube rot
Self fur ruffles citadels
Sled a tic I pit tipi
Yo yo oy oy, I O.K. koi.

I daw wadi
No sib bison
Am all llama deli
I led lamina animal
Alligator rot a gill a
Nor tap patron apron
Nor Pa defecation.
No it ace fed saga
Agas gas sag aroma amora
Mix a lot to lax,
I'm ratatat tatatar
Re-drum murder
Tiki I kit murmur
Rum rum macaroni
In or a cam
Not now won ton.

Now won rabbinical
Laci nib bar fiber
Reb if part trap patter
Ret tap teleport

Tropelet at ad data
Reel leer stops spots
On a subway yaw bus
A no sleep peels martinis
Sin I tram nut tun
A la mode operandi
I'd na repo Edom
A la walnuts stun law
Nuts stun gnus sung
Snub buns snot tons.
Bogie man name I gob
Rapper rep par ami
I'm a DJ JD.

Spin nips dial laid pun rut turn up
Marconi
In O cram mini-in I'm no Sam
Mason hero
Or eh origami,
I'm a giro
A goy yoga
I'm alas salami.

Shaman Nam ahs patron
Nor tap on no elf fur ruffle
Animal lamina
De-flip pilfered spar raps parrot tor rap.

Tom-tom mot mot
Re-drum murder red rum
Murder Nez Zen spans
Snaps I pit tipi.
Am I Kay Yakima?

Yaws sway pool loop gob bog
Gossamer REM as sog
Baffle elf fab
Amid dim a sage,

E.g. as a mall llama
I tan, I mull, I, illuminati matey
Yet am golfo
Of log golf overflow
Wolf rev O support
Trop pus sloop pools
Alias sail a net
Tab batten evasion.

No, I save revolver rev lover
Over rev O deflowered
Dere wolfed item met
I, meditator
Rot at idem moron nor om.
Aloof fool a draw yaw wayward
Live evil lived devil
Reknit tinker trap A apart.

Stink knits laced decal
Doom mood arena
An era part trap
Strap parts six ax
X-axis at ad data
Denoted detoned
A mall llama aga's saga
Sung gnus aria air
A diva avid, a ria aria
Peed deep.

A goy yoga patron
Nor tap ref log golfer
On no, a nut tuna doc cod dog god.

Spacer recaps snoops
Spoons walnuts stun laws
Woks skow folios
Soil of trader red art
Rebut tuber sugar ragus.

Star rats damned
Den mad
Stressed desserts
Doctor Rotcod.

Doctor Rotcod

Vini in IV

Enoteca acetone
Vini in IV ante Etna

Pinot nero, O rent, O nip
Garganega, age, nag, rag

Recioto oto-icer
Passito, O tis sap
Bardolino on

I, lo drab Roma Amor
An I fur Rufina

An O rev Verona
A ran it tag

Gattinara
Marsala? Alas

Ram vino di tavola
A lo vat I'd
On IV

Est Est Est tse tse tse
In IV vini

Vino on IV, a jag
Gaja

Zona an Oz C.O.D. DOC
Asti it's a) in IV

Vini enoteca acetone

Vini in IV

RV VR

Artiste et sitra
Lessuor Roussel
Noil lats
Stallion et tulo oral
La roulotte

Monaco oca nom
Maori, I roam, rev, or
Rover portable
Elba trop

La roulotte et tolu oral
No Siam maison

Stallion, noil lats Roussel, Lessour
Artiste et sitra
La roulotte et tolu oral

Monaco oca nom Nomad
Damon Tioga ago
It, Tioga, a go it sub in
I'm minibus Maori
I roam

RV VR

d'Écart traced

Écarter retrace d'écart traced émaner
Rename finit tin if mal

Lam Dada
A dad parc crap

Mais Siam éditer re: tide
Gêner, reneg, broder red orb
Le trac cartel foi
I of garçon

No crag truc curt dernier rein
Red metier re: item
Dénoter retoned déborder red-robed débuter

Retubed majeur rue jam
Par rap définitif fit
In I fed defini
In I fed pis

Sip gager re-gag
Mur rum délit tiled
Le bal label d'écart traced

d'Écart traced

Der Red

Rot tor der red
Irre err
I, Manöver rev on, am
Flug gulf Krabbe
Ebb ark flow
Rew Werwolf

Net-ad-lose-id
Die Soldaten

Was? Saw war raw?
Mähne Enham
Das sad später retaps
Tier re: it, tot tot
Das sad Ruf fur.

Atem meta Verderb bred rev
Oder redo Eiter
Re-tie husten nets
Uh
Höhe eh oh rot Tor
Der red Tor rot

Der Red

Ria Air

Ram led
Del mar días
Said sop mac

Campos on
At nap pantano
So dot todos sani-gap páginas

Eel, lee Neptuno
O nut pen rap par air tap patria

Ay alp playa
Rio de la Plata
At alp, a led oir
Maritimo

Omit? I ram Golfo of log
Mar de lodo
O doled ram
Neptuno O nut pen
Ares será ram
Mar, O crab barco

Barcelona an olé crab
Niebla Albe in ria air

Ria air

O Rue Euro

Enoteca acetone, Verderb-bred, rev
RV VR
Roussel Lessuor débuter
Retubed barco

O crab Etna, ante
Krabbe, ebb

Ark garçon
No crag Neptuno
O nut pen Marsala
Alas, ram oder redo
Émaner, rename

Será Ares Roma Amor
Atem meta dernier rein

Red niebla
Albe in Bardolino
On I, lo drab
Der red déborder red-robed
Ria air

O Rue Euro

God Dog

Ruffles self fur
Spaniel lei naps
Pug gup mug gum
Allah hall

A ruffle
Elf fur
Gnaw wang, paws
Swap Torah

Ha, rot baffle elf fab
Snap Pan's Yahweh
Hew hay, Borzoi

I, Oz, rob
Nema amen Nemo omen
Ululator rot
A lulu damned den mad dog god

Bostons snot sob superstition
No, it its rep us spans snaps
Wolf flow

Zeus Suez
Stop tops

God Dog

Mad Dam

Damn it, tin mad ria air nuts stun
Mini-in, I'm ha ha ah ah, no

Is net tension
Alligator, rot a gill, abut
Tub net tab batten
Moor room gob bog
Alias sail a tug?

Gut Ahab
Bah, a Noel lag galleon
Alee eel a
Reviver level kayak

Seep pees edit tide
Taps spat wolf flow
Woks skow stopper
Rep pots loop pool golfo

O flog at alp Plata
Re: gin Niger
Era waled Delaware
Camo top Potomac
O I ho Ohio

Hoover rev ooh Guri
I rug, no sir, rag Garrison
Aram as Samara, Gardiner
Ren I drag Tarbela

Ale brat, I, I rot
Torii mad, am madam

Mad Dam

Rail Liar

Smart trams yaw
Bus subway rail
Liar folio oil of Degas sap
Passaged elf fab baffle

Laud dual garb
Brag laid dial tor rap
Parrot rap par poseur
Rue sop tubed debut
Remit timer

Smart trams ate ETA
Spins, snips

Reb baggage car
Race gag gabber
Martini in it
Ram rat-raced decar tar
Nab, rub us suburban
Skow woks alias sail
A smart trams tram mart

Oil of folio, pilfer, reflip
Strap parts, retool looter
Noise hoc cohesion
Lab, rev verbal parrot tor rap

Rail liar
Subway yaw bus

Rail liar

(((((((((((((((((((((((((((((((( ))))))))))))))))))))))))))))))))
(((((((((((((((((((((((((((((((( ))))))))))))))))))))))))))))))))
(((((((((((((((((((((((((((((((( ))))))))))))))))))))))))))))))))
(((((((((((((((((((((((((((((((( ))))))))))))))))))))))))))))))))
(((((((((((((((((((((((((((((((( ))))))))))))))))))))))))))))))))
(((((((((((((((((((((((((((((((( ))))))))))))))))))))))))))))))))
(((((((((((((((((((((((((((((((( ))))))))))))))))))))))))))))))))
(((((((((((((((((((((((((((((((( ))))))))))))))))))))))))))))))))
(((((((((((((((((((((((((((((((( ))))))))))))))))))))))))))))))))
(((((((((((((((((((((((((((((((( ))))))))))))))))))))))))))))))))
(((((((((((((((((((((((((((((((( ))))))))))))))))))))))))))))))))
(((((((((((((((((((((((((((((((( ))))))))))))))))))))))))))))))))
(((((((((((((((((((((((((((((((( ))))))))))))))))))))))))))))))))
(((((((((((((((((((((((((((((((( ))))))))))))))))))))))))))))))))
(((((((((((((((((((((((((((((((( ))))))))))))))))))))))))))))))))
(((((((((((((((((((((((((((((((( ))))))))))))))))))))))))))))))))
(((((((((((((((((((((((((((((((( ))))))))))))))))))))))))))))))))
(((((((((((((((((((((((((((((((( ))))))))))))))))))))))))))))))))
(((((((((((((((((((((((((((((((( ))))))))))))))))))))))))))))))))
(((((((((((((((((((((((((((((((( ))))))))))))))))))))))))))))))))
(((((((((((((((((((((((((((((((( ))))))))))))))))))))))))))))))))
(((((((((((((((((((((((((((((((( ))))))))))))))))))))))))))))))))
(((((((((((((((((((((((((((((((( ))))))))))))))))))))))))))))))))
(((((((((((((((((((((((((((((((( ))))))))))))))))))))))))))))))))
(((((((((((((((((((((((((((((((( ))))))))))))))))))))))))))))))))
(((((((((((((((((((((((((((((((( ))))))))))))))))))))))))))))))))
(((((((((((((((((((((((((((((((( ))))))))))))))))))))))))))))))))
(((((((((((((((((((((((((((((((( ))))))))))))))))))))))))))))))))
(((((((((((((((((((((((((((((((( ))))))))))))))))))))))))))))))))
(((((((((((((((((((((((((((((((( ))))))))))))))))))))))))))))))))
(((((((((((((((((((((((((((((((( ))))))))))))))))))))))))))))))))
(((((((((((((((((((((((((((((((( ))))))))))))))))))))))))))))))))
(((((((((((((((((((((((((((((((( ))))))))))))))))))))))))))))))))
(((((((((((((((((((((((((((((((( ))))))))))))))))))))))))))))))))
(((((((((((((((((((((((((((((((( ))))))))))))))))))))))))))))))))
(((((((((((((((((((((((((((((((( ))))))))))))))))))))))))))))))))
(((((((((((((((((((((((((((((((( ))))))))))))))))))))))))))))))))
(((((((((((((((((((((((((((((((( ))))))))))))))))))))))))))))))))
(((((((((((((((((((((((((((((((( ))))))))))))))))))))))))))))))))
(((((((((((((((((((((((((((((((( ))))))))))))))))))))))))))))))))
(((((((((((((((((((((((((((((((( ))))))))))))))))))))))))))))))))
(((((((((((((((((((((((((((((((( ))))))))))))))))))))))))))))))))
(((((((((((((((((((((((((((((((( ))))))))))))))))))))))))))))))))
(((((((((((((((((((((((((((((((( ))))))))))))))))))))))))))))))))
(((((((((((((((((((((((((((((((( ))))))))))))))))))))))))))))))))
(((((((((((((((((((((((((((((((( ))))))))))))))))))))))))))))))))
(((((((((((((((((((((((((((((((( ))))))))))))))))))))))))))))))))

Flog Golf

Golf flog
O flog golfo, meh
Yam mayhem

Flor rolf rapper rep par O lop polo
K.O., O.K.¿

Naps span, tackle elk cat
Red rum murder
Bats stab bat tab sin
Net tennis star rats

Tar rat rat tar elf fur
Ruffle, repel leper spit on no tips

Pals slap, bonk knob raps spar rap
Par flog golf, mutilate, et. al.

It, um, gnaw wang stun nuts
Stun law walnuts wallop

Poll aw strap parts barger
Regrab embargo
O grab me

Strop ports, sports strops
Murder, re-drum, ram, mar, snip

Pins spin nips, pool, loop
O flog golfo flog golf

Flog golf

Doom Mood

Ho ho, oh oh, ha
I rap
Pariah devil
Lived torii, I, I rot

Loops spool sub bus
Nemo omen finis sin if
Spool loops dog god
DEO OED Deus sued

Tin mad, damn it
Snit tins pariah
Ha, I rap

Damned den mad
Abandon, nod, nab

A snug gun's Warsaw was raw
O rue Euro raw war dirge, e.g.
Rid O drat tardo

Pus sot tossup
Alive evil a mini-in,
I'm, I raki
Rah hari-kari

Re-drum murder red rum murder
Murmur rum rum illuminati
I tan I mull I, Warsaw, was raw

Doom mood

Esnes Sense

Sense esnes yam may
Puto or root up robalo
O labor bus sub yap pay

Rat tar tapir, rip at stink knits
Reknit tinker generous sou reneg rep aid

Diaper welfare era
Flew esne-fed defense

Burg grub Spam supper
Rep pus maps batten net tab
Ruffle elf fur

Soda ados sag gas
Snub buns, slag

Gals' ox, XO dray yard
Deliver reviled sense
Esnes' dismay, yams I'd
Dig up

Pug id or rub burro flora
A rolf dirt up putrid porcini
In I crop spin rut turnips
Animus sum in a bondage

Egad nob knar rank
Esnes sense

Esnes sense

Stressed Desserts

Gnat tang, deliver
Reviled REM may yammer rot
Cod doctor aromas, Sam

Ora embargos so grab me
Walnuts stun law, pin
Rut turnip, rebut tuber soda ados

Regal lager sugar ragus
A crab barca, a nut tuna
Pans snap tacos so cat tug gut
Stressed desserts set rot

Tortes' oil of folio
Edam made

Stressed desserts

Etna Ante

Overflow
Wolf rev

O, aval lava
Ante Etna top

Pot tap pat
Am gam magma
Isis sis I sic cis
Sicilian nail I cis
Erupter ret pure

All in wager
Re: gaw nil
Lam ire

Volcano on a clover
I'm lava
Aval sun rob
Born us

Wolf rev
Overflow

Etna ante

Animal Lamina

Oxen Nexo
Dray yard wolf
Flow dog god

Cod doc
A mall llama

Gnat tang
Parrot tor rap sung
Gnus, Elba's
Sable lee
Eel, alligator rot, a gill AA nut
Tuna

Pets step reed
Deer O
Cat taco

Animal lamina

Retroper Reporter

Sung gnus lapdog
God pal liar
Rail recap pacer
Leer, reel, edit tide

Star rats
Avid diva spool
Loops tang gnat
Flog golf star rats

Retroper reporter sung gnus
Generous sou
Reneg folio oil of
Retool looter
Straw warts lab rev

Verbal, know wonk
Star rats star

Rats retroper reporter
Per rep par rap
Deliver reviled spacer recaps
Pilfer, reflip nips
Spin parrot tor rap
Tips spit timid, dim it

Rue sop poseur
Re-drum murder

Retroper reporter
Murmur rum rum

Retroper reporter

Rotalever Revelator

Spoons snoops red now
Wonder bin nib reward
Drawer revel at or
Rotalever or eh, hero avatar

Rat Ava, I tan, I mull
I, Illuminati

Rats star, crank radial laid ark
Narc data a tad
Know wonk sung gnus
Denote e-toned straw warts

Rot sap pastor, teleport tropelet
Edit tide, emit time

Elf fab baffle
Report troper spool loops
Recap pacer, avid diva ren rut turner

I, goy yogi, spin
Nips loops spool
Rat Ava avatar traced.

Decart award, draw a rotalever revelator
Rot a lever revel at or
Decal-laced baffle elf fab

I, maw's swami, spool loops
Laid dial lap pal spin nips
Rotalever Revalator illuminati
I tan, I mull, I or eh hero
No Sam Mason

Rotalever Revelator

god lived as a devil dog
lived as a devil dog god
as a devil dog god lived
a devil dog god lived as
devil dog god lived as a
dog god lived as a devil
god lived as a devil dog
lived as a devil dog god
as a devil dog god lived
a devil dog god lived as
devil dog god lived as a
dog god lived as a devil
god lived as a devil dog
lived as a devil dog god
as a devil dog god lived
a devil dog god lived as
devil dog god lived as a
dog god lived as a devil
god lived as a devil dog
lived as a devil dog god
as a devil dog god lived
a devil dog god lived as
devil dog god lived as a
dog god lived as a devil
god lived as a devil dog
lived as a devil dog god
as a devil dog god lived
a devil dog god lived as
devil dog god lived as a
god lived as a devil dog
lived as a devil dog god
as a devil dog god lived
a devil dog god lived as
devil dog god lived as a
dog god lived as a devil
god lived as a devil dog
lived as a devil dog god
as a devil dog god lived
a devil dog god lived as
devil dog god lived as a
dog god lived as a devil
god lived as a devil dog
lived as a devil dog god
as a devil dog god lived
a devil dog god lived as
devil dog god lived as a
dog god lived as a devil
god lived as a devil dog
lived as a devil dog god
as a devil dog god lived
a devil dog god lived as
devil dog god lived as a
dog god lived as a devil
god lived as a devil dog
lived as a devil dog god
as a devil dog god lived
a devil dog god lived as
devil dog god lived as a
dog god lived as a devil
god lived as a devil dog